Help the Bear

Jeremy Caliz

Presentation by *BookLeaf Publishing*

Web: www.bookleafpub.com

E-mail: info@bookleafpub.com

ISBN: 9789357740470

First edition 2023

This book is dedicated to those who helped me along with this writing business. Starting with my Mom who gave me my first journal, all the teachers(who need more money and benefits)that showed me how to use language to communicate my inner feelings, my Dad who taught me to read everything and never shaded my interests. My brothers Henny, Ripp, K, Dro, and Dramie who let me rap with them. The homies P, Flow, Marx, Black and Damian for their willingness to accept me as their friend. The Brothers in Crimson and Grey. Thanks to Donna and Joni and Gerald and that whole English department. To my beloved wife, thanks for everything Big Guy.

ACKNOWLEDGEMENT

S/o to God the Father, God the Son and God the Holy Spirit. Shout to the Wisdom. Peace to the family and the homies. Even more peace to the enemies, both deserved and undeserved.

PREFACE

The idea behind this is doing a favor for my self from 10-12ish years ago. That guy went-put himself through-some things and started writing. Prayers and poems and lyrics and lists, maybe there isn't much difference between these when what's needed is to get the shit out. Anyhoodles, I thought that he should have a break and this is it.

May 10, 2021

I was laying in bed, thinking of ending it all.

We knew it hadn't worked
all the shows and sights
every all you could eat-not the shrimp-
Failure.

Boredom's dry heat
insulated the solitude.

She was the planner.

The night before the flight out
I was in the guest room. I heard them and it
didn't matter.

I wonder who saw us in that mall of a city,
feeling in the dark...

Passing

I remember the party.

Damp walls and air conditioning.

Cake and old Black Women
arranged like so much furniture.

Me and my niggas
didn't belong in that tight living room.

The boy stopped
His gaze was fingers snapping, reaching for the
owner of that face. That laugh.

Eyes wide and joyful as we have the catch fade
defeated when gathered away at bedtime.

No story.

No hug leaving a trail to follow all the
tomorrows when I won't return.

Again.

I wonder if I'll ever meet him;
whoever he thought I was.

Eastern Promises

Riding into the Sun/Away from home-

At home on the rail
The nurse and the vagrant
A laborer
An owner
Expecting the dream's fruition.

All lives matter-theories are relative

Sleepovers for the kids/Community bylaws
protect the avarice
Summer camps arm your daughters Civilize the
savages

Another train tripping dollar search/Cotton
Dockers in
Parking Spaces
Wandering wayfarers
Trust no one, believe yourself-yourself-

Ambition is my ammunition/the homeless hit the
floor

Living the policy-victims of poverty

And with my lips I kiss the Lord/good Christian

Good Christian...

Good Christian.

Eastern Promises/Eastern Promises-no doubt
indeed-

Eastern Promises/Eastern Promises

Grief

I could have known you on those nights when
we were men-briefly-
our difference of degree and not kind.
Those nights too late to be early, we bore our
burden to the river.

Surrounded as we were by the fires; Flat light
brightening nothing, we saw through dim plastic
the symbols of our sentiments.

Washing out the fear and the days, the silent
screams of a man under water, wrung out.

There we paid time to take time away in that
dirty lobby, the only place that felt clean.

No confessions. No lessons. Nothing.

Just us doing laundry on Hillside Ave at 3 a.m.

Almost Lover

At the corner of Jamaica and Francis Lewis, I
looked south and saw you.

Milk brown skin and red curls.
Freckled face, promising hips.

I was too stupid.

I thought I missed you,
my reckless illusion of pure love.

You were always your own; that made you
irresistible.

June 20, 2017

A plane across the sky, pearls on a silver tray
versus the late burning sun and dripping clouds.

It passes as through dimensions, unreasonably,
shrugging off time, tail lights glittering.

Not Haiku

1.

Slowly after
style degenerated,
apathy set in.

2.

Time travel was my
escape route with
no paradoxes.

3.

A universe, if,
divided against
self, will lemon curry?

Views

Out the window, stage left

Across from the woman most closely resembling
my Sister

To the right of the man with the shirt
The man whose eyes see niggers
when he comes to my City.

The servant

curled in the seat

bullshitting in drowsy Spanish,
her head balanced on the cushion

while my childhood passed us by.

Under the Current

I wonder if Batman cries

At daybreak, the warm sun revealing the dust
and neglect and

disinfecting the wounds of bad jokes and broken
hearts.

Does Batman sob deeply

in the winelight, a memory of truffles and paté
mixing with his tears...

Will Batman weep loudly without shame,

Lonely-not alone- in his gilded Batcave, alive
with machines, uncontaminated by love

And does Alfred, hearing,
quake with sympathy for his son-not son-
Or become scarce, washing -and washing-
dishes worn ever smoother under the current of
his resigned fate?

May 23, 2017

In more parts present than missing,

I am a man

For a moment.

In the half sun that late morning,
among the highborn and their low expectations
of us,

The killer's glance reminded me of what was
missed.

And who wouldn't be.

Dream

Sidestep parry right-

Forward lunge

slash.

-Down arm, clench tight

index middle ring edge;

Look up-

Watch life,

universe and sky

cracking, quaking, creaking

The funneled running time always full, direction
varied,

its destination certain-

The enemy's thoughts are his destiny.

The eye trails the haze.

A heron penetrates the glass.

Not Haiku

1.

The pain of the win

is to die. The agony of

defeat is to live.

2.

How often is a

day passing by when the cool

of dawn fades to red?

Not Really

Let it never be said,

when it's time to start saying,

I was a good man.

Too much truth sours the wine.

Child

Be available for less,

Sleep in for more.

Grief

Two weeks ago,

on the way home,

I'd forgotten

that West died.

Drankin

The streets were crowded

with the huddled masses.

I and I

oil in this sea of jagged memories.

There was one, stooped over his spilled

wallet and pocket contents.

I didn't look closely at the shifting

air holding his fractal un-motion.

What was it I felt,
not watching this crossroads reveal itself?

I could not have looked back

at foggy windows,

buckling floor,

and creaking roof.

I refused to remember

the too high seats,

that hateful fuzz of a sour dawn's

broken promises.

I had to reach my destination,

wherever it is.

February 13, 2023

-Let me hear somethin-

Yo,
I'm not all about them streets
where I fought so hard
for my fans to keep my words
like I crossed yo heart

-wait...did you see the lookbook? Lotsa
denims...I know...-

Should I keep going?
I approach beats with my teeth showing
flowing machine from
East of the East

-oh my God another baby! Love that for them-

hocus pocus your hopes
are hopeless homie
keep it peace or the piece blowing-

so what's my exposure here...but we had a
contract.

You're doing great!-

I see everything
man analyzes nuance
waited too long to move on
   out with the old shit
/time/to get my new on

It's cold in the Triple D, my nigga,
keep ya shoes on
no spittin lukewarm
them type of lies we
beat the truth from

-that might be cool for that OTHER show. Who
else do we-

This is all an act
I looked up to "killers" when I rapped
now I'm stuck on this DVD
talkin Smack
minerals and vitamins I lack
only fortified with the 45 pointed at my back
Big dick playa, wish I was strapped...

-Thanks for coming in, we'll be in touch.

NEXT!-

The title of this poem is what you're reading right now.

Day passes into day,
Head bowed and body softened;

the sweets won't let me chill.

A metal shipping container full
Of frightened employees,
I am one of those.

Long stockinged and jacketed,
bag heavy with the remains of the day,
Tempered as the glass.

In all this running time;

I deeply yearn for Summer.

The Cat Bits

People love cats

those independent badasses.

Yes you do. They say cats are

funny and smart

                      -my cat cried and it made
me cry-

how cohyute.

We love cats
so much we name all our stuff after them.

I'm gonna rest
catnap
Give directions

                    -it's kitty-corner to the sneaker
spot-

If you're under 40 and say kitty-corner in 2019 I
don't trust you.

Cats are
named for all the bad stuff too.

Catastrophe
Cataclysm

                    -#college much?-

The Bible says:
Jesus was beaten with a Cat o Nine tails.

My nigga,
I see a 9 tailed cat I'm leaving the planet.

Asshole Bestie

And so we teased and mocked with

our laughter coated shame and fear

in the early night's sun.

The cold wasn't yet stinging

even that early in November

October

she drove that day.

They paid.

I read a book about Asians.

She was right.

When she saw me in that suit later,

hair laid, lines sharp

had I been able to hold it together?

She was right.

Everything sheds and on and on

What were we supposed to do?

I had always been letting her down;

We made no place for her.

Among the Breezes

A loose gang of birds

on the platform pecked

for stones.

Good morning, the greeting and request.
A coin, the price and possession.

The wind like a dog's threat,
dust stinging my eyes at its coming,
that great sky serpent.

It was then, among the breezes,
that I thought of sleeping next to you.

February 4th, 2017

I was asleep this morning and had a vision.

Perched on the bridge like some kind of

superhero for bitch niggas.

I felt the water snap my spinal cord.

The Creator, I call Father with my lips.

Does my life do the same?

I read

the cynic finds no joy because he can no longer

be surprised.

Which of you diversions stole my curiosity?

I can hear HIS silence.

7th Grade was bully season.

I wrote dark things no one saw.

The gang homies taught me my life wasn't worth
risking.

I felt my mind slip.

I sense no future beyond Christmas.

Jamison said this is what it is:

the struggle and the return.

Wake up away from the edge,

pray for a new mind,

wait til tomorrow.